HCG Approved Slow Cooker Recipes: Lose Weight Quickly With These Low Carb Options on the HCG Diet

Disclaimer and Terms of Use: Effort has been made to ensure that the information in this book is accurate and complete, however, the author and the publisher do not warrant the accuracy of the information, text and graphics contained within the book due to the rapidly changing nature of science, research, known and unknown facts and Internet. The Author and the publisher do not hold any responsibility for errors, omissions or contrary interpretation of the subject matter herein. This book is presented solely for motivational and informational purposes only.

Table of Contents

Fall Harvest Cake 33

Bacon Chicken Chowder

Ingredients:
- 4 T minced garlic
- 1 shallot, diced
- 2 celery stalks, diced
- 1 can diced mushrooms
- 1 sweet onion, chopped
- 4 T butter
- 2 C chicken broth
- 1 lb. chicken breast
- 8 oz. cream cheese
- 1 C heavy cream
- 1 lb. cooked bacon, crumbled
- 1 tsp. salt and pepper
- 1 tsp. garlic powder
- 1 tsp. thyme

Directions:

I.   Set your slow cooker to the lowest setting
II.   Add all your seasonings and vegetables to the slow cooker with the broth and cook on low for 1 hour
III.   Cook your chicken on all sides in a skillet with a little butter; you're just searing, not cooking thoroughly
IV.   Dice chicken and add this and the bacon crumbs to your slow cooker
V.   Cook for remaining 6-8 hours on low

Jerk Chicken

Ingredients:
- 8 scallions, chopped
- ¼ C vegetable oil
- 2 habanero chilies, seeded and chopped
- 2 T molasses
- 3 T minced garlic
- 1 thyme
- 2 tsp. allspice
- ¼ tsp. cardamom
- 1 tsp. salt and pepper to taste
- 4 lbs. chicken, sliced

Directions:

I. Add the first nine ingredients and your salt to a food processor or blender and puree
II. Add ½ C of this to your slow cooker
III. Add the chicken to the slow cooker and coat with the mixture and cook for 4-6 hours
IV. Place remaining puree in the fridge until ready to use
V. Set your oven rack 10" from the broiler setting in oven and set to broil
VI. Add chicken, lined on foil, to the broiler rack and brush remaining puree mix on each side of chicken, broil for 8-10 minutes on each side
VII. Serve

Shredded Beef and Cabbage

Ingredients:
- 2 lbs. beef, trimmed
- 1 T taco seasoning
- 3 T olive oil
- 2 cans chilies

Cabbage Dressing

- 1 head green cabbage
- ½ head red cabbage
- ½ C green onion, sliced
- 6 T light mayo
- 4 tsp. lime juice
- 2 tsp. green tabasco sauce

Avocado salsa

- 2 diced avocados
- 1 poblano pepper, diced
- 1 T lime juice
- 1 T EVOO
- ½ C chopped cilantro

Directions:
I. Rub your beef in the taco seasoning, then cut into strips
II. Heat in a skillet on all sides, to sear
III. Add the seared strips into your slow cooker with the diced chilies and juices
IV. Cook on high for 4 hours; you want the meat to shred apart easily
V. Shred the meat and leave in the cooker to stay warm
VI. Prepare your cabbage and salsa
VII. Slice your cabbage into strips and slice your onions

VIII.   Whisk other cabbage ingredients together for the dressing and toss the cabbage and onions with the dressing
IX.   Whisk the salsa together as well or blend
X.   Layer your dish with the slaw, then beef, and salsa

HCG Stuffed Peppers

Ingredients:
- 1 lb. ground sausage
- 2 green peppers
- 2 red peppers
- 1 yellow pepper
- ½ head cauliflower, chopped
- 1 can tomato paste
- 1 white onion, diced
- 2 T minced garlic
- 2 tsp. dried basil
- 2 tsp. oregano
- 2 tsp. thyme

Directions:

I. Halve and scoop out the peppers but save your tops
II. Process the cauliflower into rice and set aside in small bowl
III. Add remaining seasonings to the cauliflower and stir
IV. Brown the sausage in a skillet, a good searing or browning
V. Add rest of ingredients with the sausage to the remaining mixture in your bowl
VI. Spoon this into the peppers evenly
VII. Add 1-2 T of water to the bottom of your slow cooker to keep it from burning the bottoms of your peppers
VIII. Add peppers to bottom of slow cooker in the water
IX. Cook on low for 4-6 hours

Zucchini Meatloaf

Ingredients:
- 2 lbs. ground beef
- 2 eggs
- 1 C shredded zucchini
- 1/2 C parmesan cheese
- 1 1/2 C Italian parsley
- 4 T minced garlic
- 3 T balsamic vinegar
- 1 T oregano
- 2 T minced onion
- 1/2 tsp. salt and pepper to taste

Topping

- 1/4 C ketchup
- 1/4 C mozzarella cheese
- 2 T Italian parsley

Directions:

I. Mix everything in a mixing bowl for your meatloaf and form a loaf with your hands
II. Add foil to the bottom of the slow cooker
III. Add loaf to the bottom of the foil and fold in around the loaf
IV. Cook for 6 hours on low
V. Add toppings over loaf and cook another 10 minutes

Bologna Cauliflower

Ingredients:
- 1 head cauliflower
- ¾ C diced onion
- 2 T minced garlic
- 2 tsp. dried oregano flakes
- 1 tsp. basil
- 2 cans diced tomatoes
- ½ C vegetable broth
- ¼ tsp. red pepper flakes
- salt and pepper to taste
- 5-6 zucchinis, shredded

Directions:

I. Add everything for the bolognas into the slow cooker and cook for 3 ½ hours on high
II. Mash cauliflower until it creates bologna
III. Spoon over the noodles

Crockpot Lasagna

Ingredients:
Marinara:

- ¼ C olive oil
- 1 diced onion
- 1 tsp. salt
- 1 tsp. minced garlic
- 7 tomatoes
- ½ tsp. honey

Meat:

- 1 T olive oil
- ½ diced onion
- 1 lb. ground turkey
- ½ tsp. salt and pepper to taste
- 18 chopped basil leaves

Cheese:

- ½ tsp. olive oil
- ¼ small onion, chopped
- ½ squash, chopped
- ½ tsp. minced garlic
- ¼ tsp. salt and pepper to taste
- ½ C coconut milk
- 1 egg
- 4 medium zucchinis

Directions:

I.   Heat your skillet with oil and brown the ground turkey
II. Then add in your salt and pepper making sure that everything is well blended
III. You will assemble this as you would any other lasagna

IV.   Your zucchini needs to be sliced length wise for your lasagna noodles
V.   Whisk your sauce in a sauce pan
VI.   Layer lasagna in slow cooker
VII.   Cook on low for 1 ½ hours
VIII. You will pour sauce over LAST

Squash and Meatballs

Ingredients:

- spaghetti squash
- 1 lb. ground sausage
- 1 can tomato sauce
- 2 T red pepper relish
- 5 T minced garlic
- 2 T olive oil
- 2 tsp. Italian seasoning

Directions:

I. Dump the seasoning and tomato sauce into your slow cooker and stir
II. Halve your squash and scoop out any seeds
III. Add the squash to the slow cooker, face down
IV. Roll the meat into meatballs and fit them down into the slow cooker with the squash and sauce
V. Cook on low for 5-6 hours
VI. Serve

Heart Healthy Beef Stew

Ingredients:
- 2 lbs. beef stew meat
- 3 T olive oil
- 2 C beef stock (organic is best)
- ½ lb. bacon crumbs
- 1 can diced tomatoes with chilies
- mixed bell peppers (one of each)
- 1 can chopped mushrooms
- 2 celery sticks, chopped
- 1 carrot, chopped
- 1 onion, chopped
- 4 T minced garlic
- 2 T tomato paste
- 2 T coconut amino
- 2 tsp. salt and pepper to taste
- 1 ½ tsp. garlic powder
- 1 tsp. onion powder
- 1 tsp. dried oregano

Directions:

I.   Set to slowest setting on your slow cooker
II.   Sear your vegetables and beef over low heat in a skillet, than set in slow cooker
III. Add rest of ingredients to slow cooker
IV.   Cook on low with lid for 8 hours

Roasted Chicken and Gravy

Ingredients:

- 4-5 lbs. chicken (whole or breasts)
- 2 T ghee
- 2 onions, chopped
- 6 T minced garlic
- 1 tsp. tomato paste
- ¼ C chicken broth
- ¼ C white wine
- seasoning
- salt and pepper to taste

Directions:

I. Chop your vegetables
II. Sauté them with the garlic on a large skillet
III. Stir in the tomato paste
IV. Transfer over to your slow cooker with seasonings
V. Add your chicken to the slow cooker
VI. Cook on low for 4-6 hours
VII. Take bird out for the juices, let it sit for about 20 minutes, to get as many juices from the bird as you can; this is where your gravy flavor will come from
VIII. Use an immersion blender for your gravy
IX. Shred chicken or serve in larger pieces
X. Serve with your homemade chicken gravy

Stuffed Greek Chicken

Ingredients:
- 2 lbs. chicken breasts
- 3 C spinach, chopped
- 2 bell peppers, chopped
- ¼ C black olives
- 1 C artichoke hearts
- 4 oz. pkg. feta cheese
- 1 T oregano, chopped
- 1 tsp. garlic powder
- 1 ½ C chicken broth
- salt and pepper to taste

Directions:

I.   Mix your vegetables, feta and two seasonings
II. Season your chicken to taste
III. Cut deep slit in chicken and stuff with spinach blend
IV. Set in slow cooker, slit end up
V.   Pour in chicken broth carefully
VI. Cook on low for 4 hours

Mole Chicken

Ingredients:
- 2 lbs. chicken pieces
- salt and pepper to taste
- 2 T ghee
- 1 onion, chopped
- 4 T minced garlic
- 6 whole tomatoes, seeded and chopped
- 5 sun dried chili peppers, chopped
- ¼ C almond butter
- 2 ½ oz. dark chocolate chips
- 1 tsp. cumin powder
- ½ tsp. cinnamon powder
- ½ tsp. guajillo chili powder
- cilantro, avocado and jalapenos and chopped

Directions:

I. Season your chicken to taste with salt and pepper
II. In a pan, heat the ghee and chicken until brown all around
III. Transfer over to slow cooker and add onions and sauté
IV. Add in garlic
V. Add these to the slow cooker and remaining ingredients
VI. Cook on low for 6 hours
VII. Top with last set of three ingredients
VIII. Serve

Crockpot Chili

Ingredients:
- 2 lbs. ground beef
- diced onion
- 3 T minced garlic
- 1 red pepper, chopped
- 1 green pepper, chopped
- 1 C carrots, chopped
- 1 jalapeno, chopped
- 1 can crushed stewed tomatoes
- 1 can diced tomatoes
- 3 T chili powder
- 1 T oregano
- 1 T basil
- 2 tsp. cumin
- 1 tsp. salt and pepper to taste
- 1 tsp. onion powder
- ½ tsp. cayenne
- 1 T bacon crumbs
- 1 avocado, diced

Directions:

I. Start with sautéing your vegetables and garlic over medium heat

II. Add in the beef, browning, and get rid of all the excess fat

III. Transfer everything over to your slow cooker and cook on low for 6 hours

IV. Serve hot with avocado and bacon to garnish

Beef and Cabbage

Ingredients:
- ½ lb. baby carrots
- 2 onions, chopped
- 1 cabbage, small, wedged
- 8 T minced garlic
- bay leaf
- 2 center cut shanks
- salt and pepper to taste
- 1 ½ oz. can diced tomatoes
- 1 C chicken broth
- 2 T coconut amino

Directions:

I. Add all of your vegetables to your slow cooker, along with the seasonings, and broth

II. Sear your meat in a skillet over medium heat until seared on each side

III. Add to your slow cooker and cook for 8-9 hours on low

Meatball Soup

Ingredients:

- 2 cans beef stock
- 1 zucchini, chopped
- 2 ribs celery, chopped
- 1 can tomato, diced
- 1 ½ T minced garlic
- 1 ½ lbs. ground beef
- 1 egg
- 4 T chopped parsley
- 1 ½ tsp. onion powder
- salt and pepper to taste

Directions:

I.   Set your slow cooker to lowest setting and add your stock and vegetables
II. Blend your beef, and other remaining ingredients until well mixed and create 25-30 meatballs with your hands
III. Brown meatballs over heat in a skillet, then add them to your slow cooker
IV. Cook on low for 6 hours

HCG Slow Cooker Desserts

Triple Berry Cobbler

Ingredients:
- 1 C flour
- ¾ C sugar
- 1 tsp. baking powder
- ¼ tsp. ground cinnamon
- ¼ tsp. nutmeg
- 2 eggs, whisked
- 2 T vegetable oil
- 2 T milk
- 2 C blueberries
- 2 C raspberries
- 2 C blackberries
- 1 C sugar
- 1 C water
- 3 T tapioca

Directions:

I.   In one bowl sift dry ingredients, and add in whisked eggs
II. In saucepan, add berries and 1 C sugar and tapioca, let boil
III. Pour hot fruit mixture into slow cooker and spoon batter over top
IV. Cook on high 1 ½ hours, maybe 2 as needed
V.   Turn off slow cooker after final hour and let SIT IN SLOW COOKER for another hour to settle and cool

Crockpot Cinnamon Rolls

Ingredients:
- 2 can Crescent rolls
- ½ C cinnamon chips
- 4 T butter
- ½ C sugar
- 1 tsp. ground cinnamon

Directions:

I.   Spray your slow cooker with nonstick spray

II.   Sift the cinnamon and sugar together

III.   Add the cinnamon chips to your unrolled crescent rolls

IV.   Reroll the rolls and pinch edges to close

V.   Dip each roll into the sugar and cinnamon and set in slow cooker

VI.   Pour melted butter over rolls, in the slow cooker

VII.   Cook on low for 2 hours

HCG Pecan Pie

Ingredients:
- 1 premade pie crust
- 3 eggs
- 1 C sugar
- 2/3 C Karo syrup
- 1 C pecans, halves or crushed
- 1/2 C melted butter
- 1 tsp. vanilla

Directions:

I. Start with spraying your slow cooker
II. Lay the premade crust along the bottom, and up the edges, about ½ - 1" or so
III. Blend your remaining ingredients in a mixing bowl on low to medium
IV. Pour into your slow cooker over the crust
V. Cook on high for 2 ½ hours

3 Layer Brownies

Ingredients:
- 1 ¼ C almond flour
- ¼ C cocoa powder
- ¾ tsp. baking powder
- ½ tsp. sea salt
- ½ C low sodium butter
- 1 pkg. chocolate chips
- 1 C raw sugar
- 3 eggs, whisked
- 1 C walnut halves
- 1 C semi-sweet chocolate chips

Directions:

I.   Grease or spray your slow cooker edges
II.   In a bowl, whisk your dry ingredients
III.   In separate microwave safe bowl, melt the butter and bittersweet chocolate chips
IV.   Add the dry ingredients to the bowl and stir in your eggs
V.   Add remaining ingredients
VI.   Stir and pour into slow cooker
VII.   Cook covered on low for 3 ½ hours
VIII.   Remove lid and cook for another 30 minutes
IX.   Let cool for about 2 hours before serving

Molten Lava Cake

Ingredients:
- 1 C almond flour
- 2 tsp. baking powder
- 6 T low sodium butter
- 1/3 C chocolate chips
- 1 C sugar
- 3 T + 1/3 C sugar
- 1 T vanilla
- 1/4 tsp salt
- 1/3 C almond milk
- 1 egg yolk
- 1/3 C brown sugar
- 1 1/2 C hot water

Directions:

I. Spray the inside of your slow cooker
II. Sift the dry ingredients in a bowl and set aside
III. In separate bowl, melt the chocolate chips and butter
IV. Stir in remaining ingredients
V. Stir both bowls together
VI. Pour batter in to the slow cooker
VII. Cook on high for 1-2 hours

The Shirley Temple

Ingredients:
- 1 box French Vanilla cake mix
- 1 C sprite
- 3 beaten eggs
- ¼ C vegetable oil
- ¼ C cherry juice
- 1 jar maraschino cherries

Frosting

- 1 tsp. vanilla
- 1 box powdered sugar
- 1 stick butter (low sodium)
- 1/3 C maraschino cherry juice

Directions

I.   In bowl mix everything together and mix well
II.   Spray your slow cooker from the bottom up
III. Pour in the cake batter
IV.   Cook on high for 2 - 2 ½ hours
V.   Take the lid off and let cook
VI.   Flip out of the bowl let cook
VII. Frost then add cherry juice over top

For your frosting:

Beat the frosting ingredients together until smooth

Chocolate Peanut Butter Cake

Ingredients:

- ½ C low sodium butter
- ½ C raw sugar or substitute
- ½ C brown sugar
- 3 eggs, whisked
- ½ C Nutella
- ¾ C light sour cream
- 1 tsp. Vanilla
- 2 ½ C almond flour
- 1 tsp. baking powder
- ½ tsp. salt
- 1 C chocolate chips

Directions:

I.   Cream your butter, sugar, eggs, peanut butter (Nutella) and vanilla
II. Add the dry ingredients in one at a time, stirring consistently
III. Use most of the chocolate chips, but you can save some for the top
IV. Pour or spoon into your slow cooker
V.   Cook on high for 3-4 hours

Turtle Pudding

Ingredients:
- 1 1/2 C Bisquick
- 1 C brown sugar
- 1/2 C cocoa powder
- 1/2 C almond milk
- 1/4 C Caramel sauce
- 1 2/3 C hot water
- 1/2 C chopped pecans

Directions:

I. Spray your slow cooker down with nonstick spray
II. Add everything but your hot water into a mixing bowl and blend well
III. Pour into slow cooker
IV. Pour hot water over batter but DO NOT STIR
V. Cover and cook for 2 ½ Hours
VI. Let cool
VII. Serve

Lemon Cake

Ingredients:
- 1 ¾ C almond flour
- ½ C cornmeal
- 1 tsp. baking powder
- 1 tsp. baking soda
- ¼ tsp. sea salt
- 1 ½ stick butter, warm
- 1 ¼ C sugar
- 2 eggs
- 1 C low fat sour cream
- ½ tsp. vanilla
- 1 T lemon zest + 3 T lemon juice
- 1 tsp. poppy seeds
- 1 T powdered sugar

Directions:

I.   In one bowl sift your dry ingredients
II.   In a mixing bowl blend your eggs, sugar and remaining wet ingredients
III.   Combine two bowls of ingredients
IV.   Pour mixture into slow cooker and cook for 2 ½ hours
V.   Let sit for 15 minutes before serving

Fall Harvest Cake

Ingredients:
- 2 cans sliced apples
- 1 spice cake mix
- ½ C melted butter
- ½ C chopped pecans

Directions:

I.   Spray the slow cooker with nonstick spray
II.   Dump the apples and juices from can into slow cooker
III.   Top with cake mix
IV.   Pour apple butter over mix and sprinkle with pecans
V.   Cook for 4 hours
VI.   Serve warm, goes great with Phase 1 ice cream

Made in the USA
Middletown, DE
17 January 2022